I0477015

Skulls
Day of the Dead A Stress Management Coloring Books for Grown-Ups

Adult Coloring Book J. Kaiwell
And
John Daniel

Published by PUBLISHING COMPANY in 2016
First edition: First printing

allcoloringbook.com

ISBN-13: 978-1523425488
ISBN-10: 1523425482

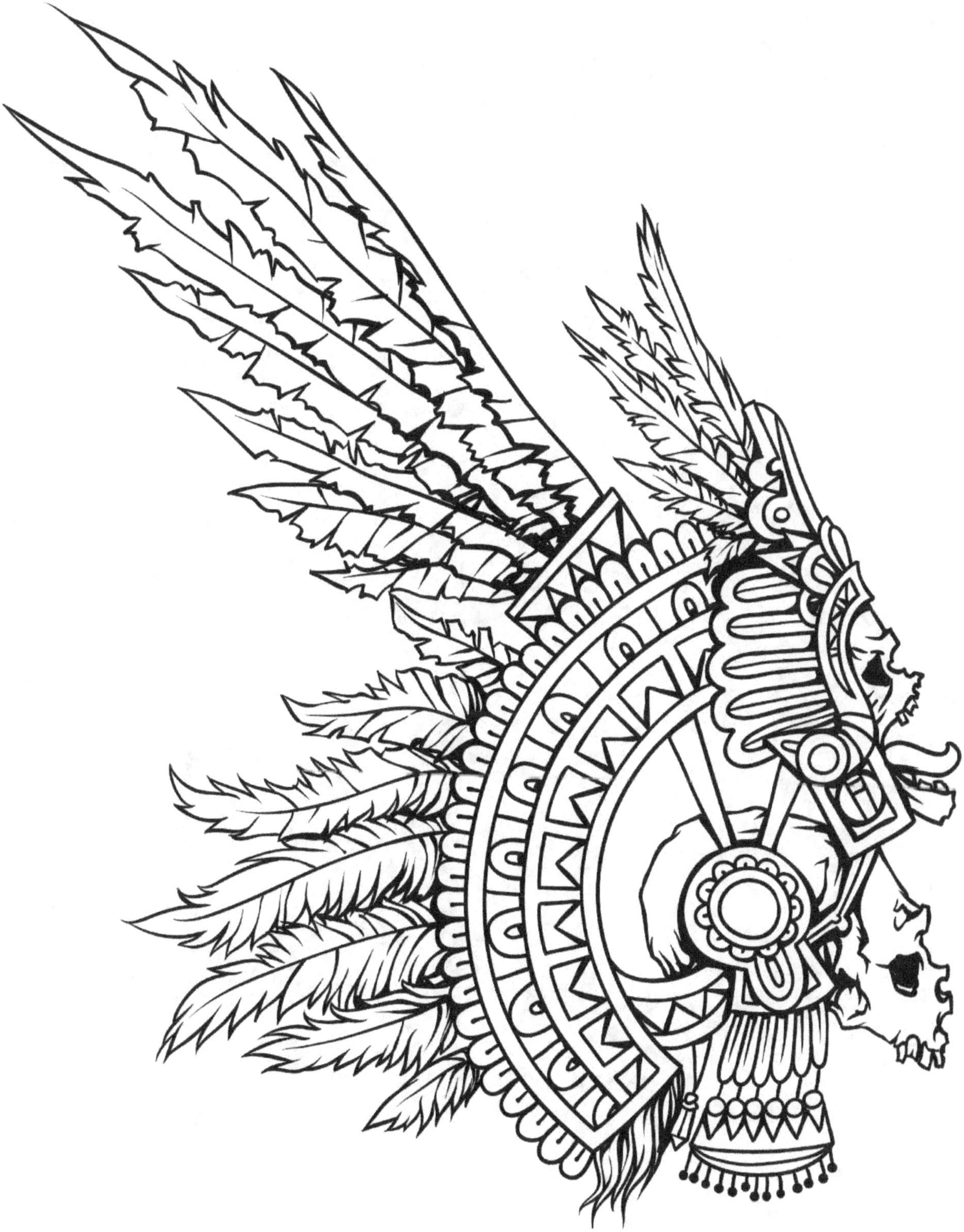

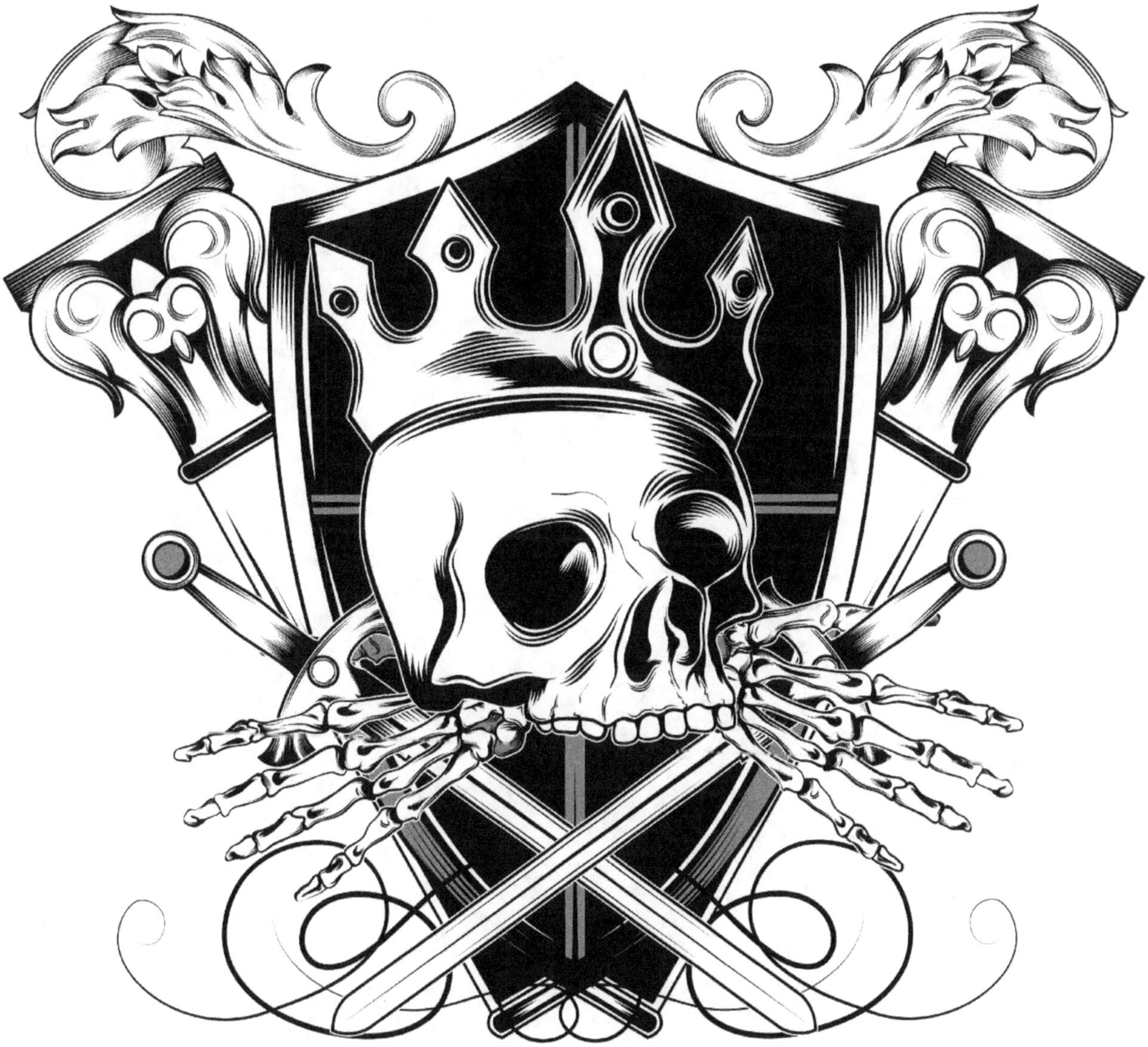

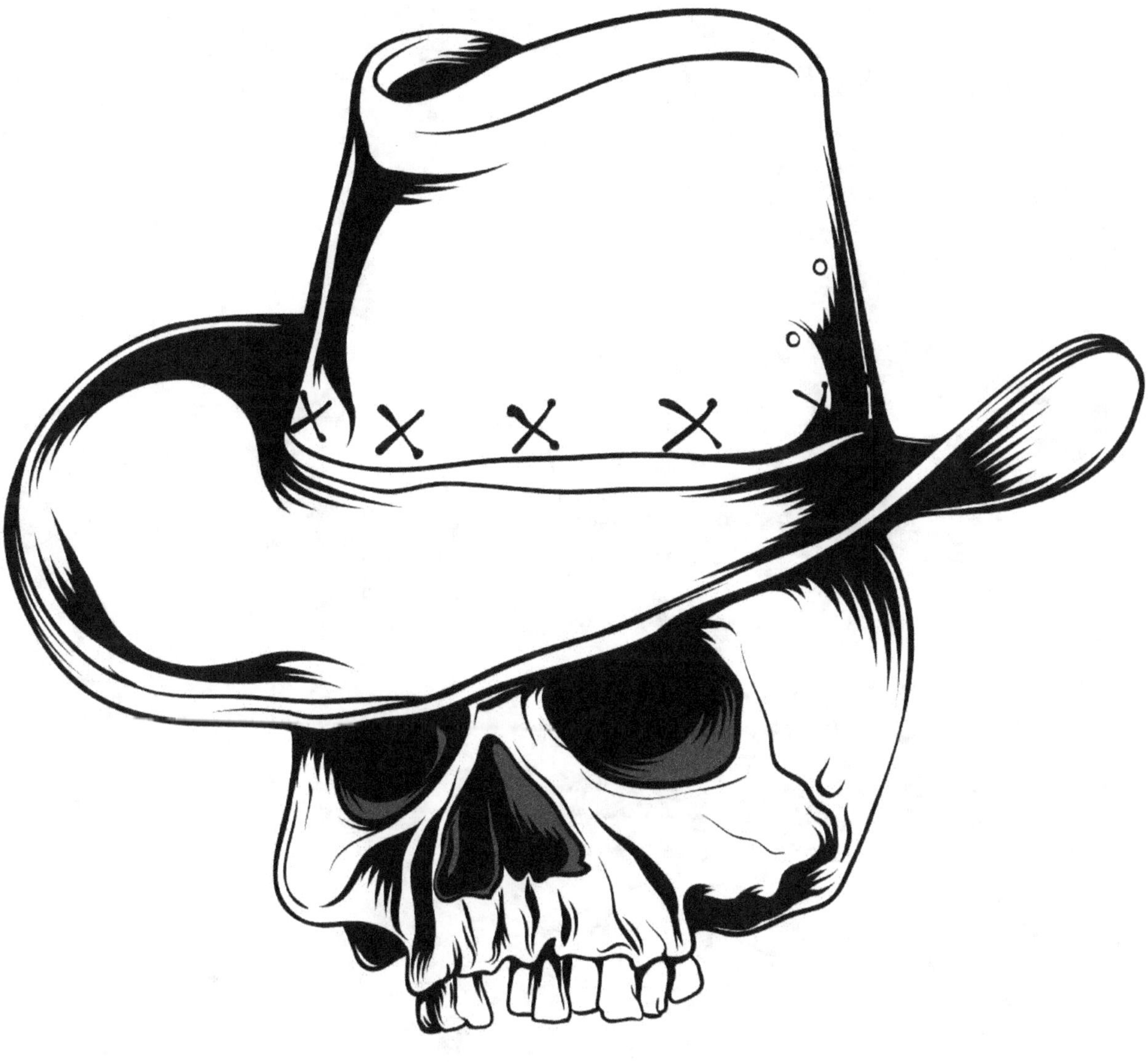

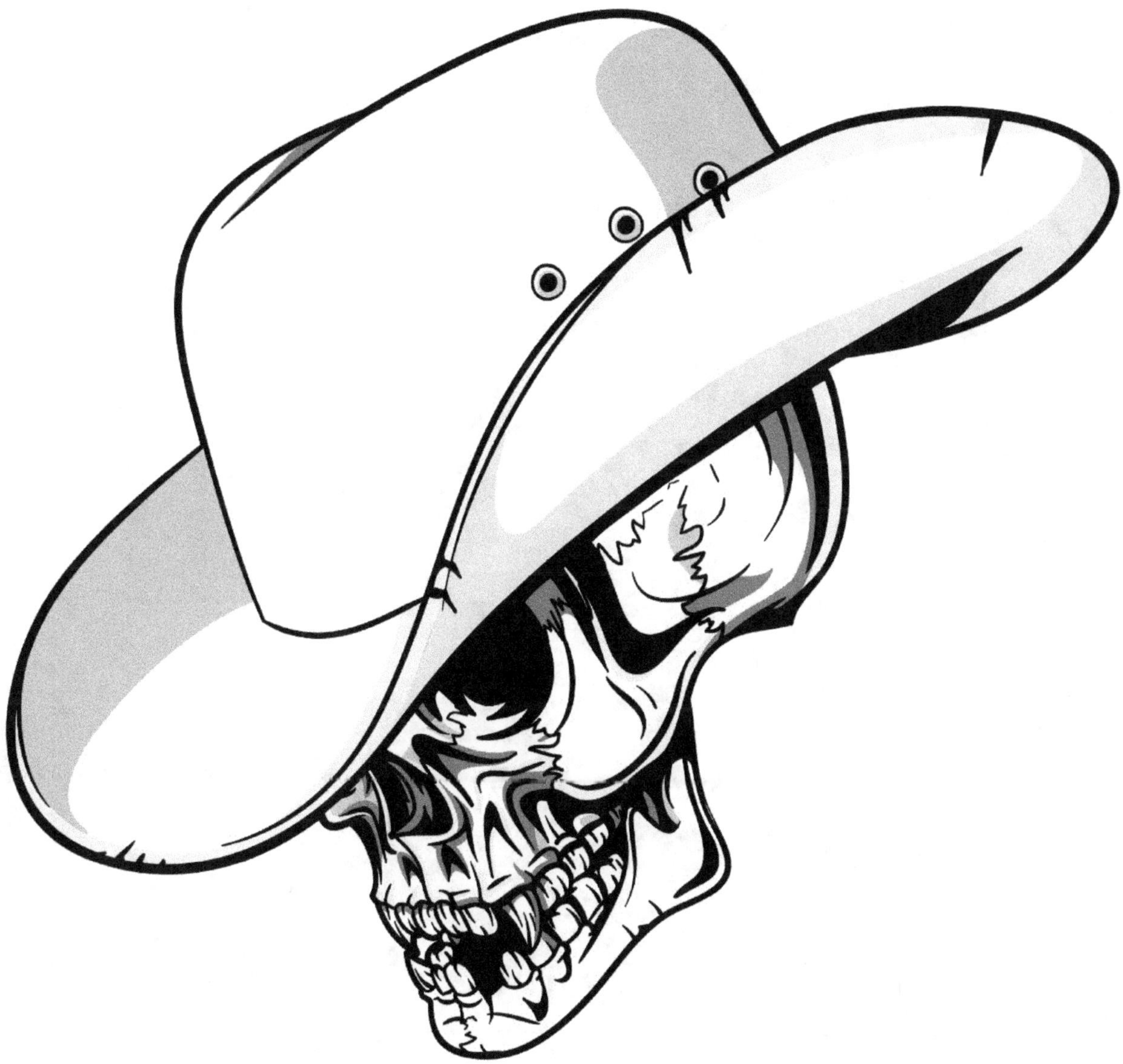

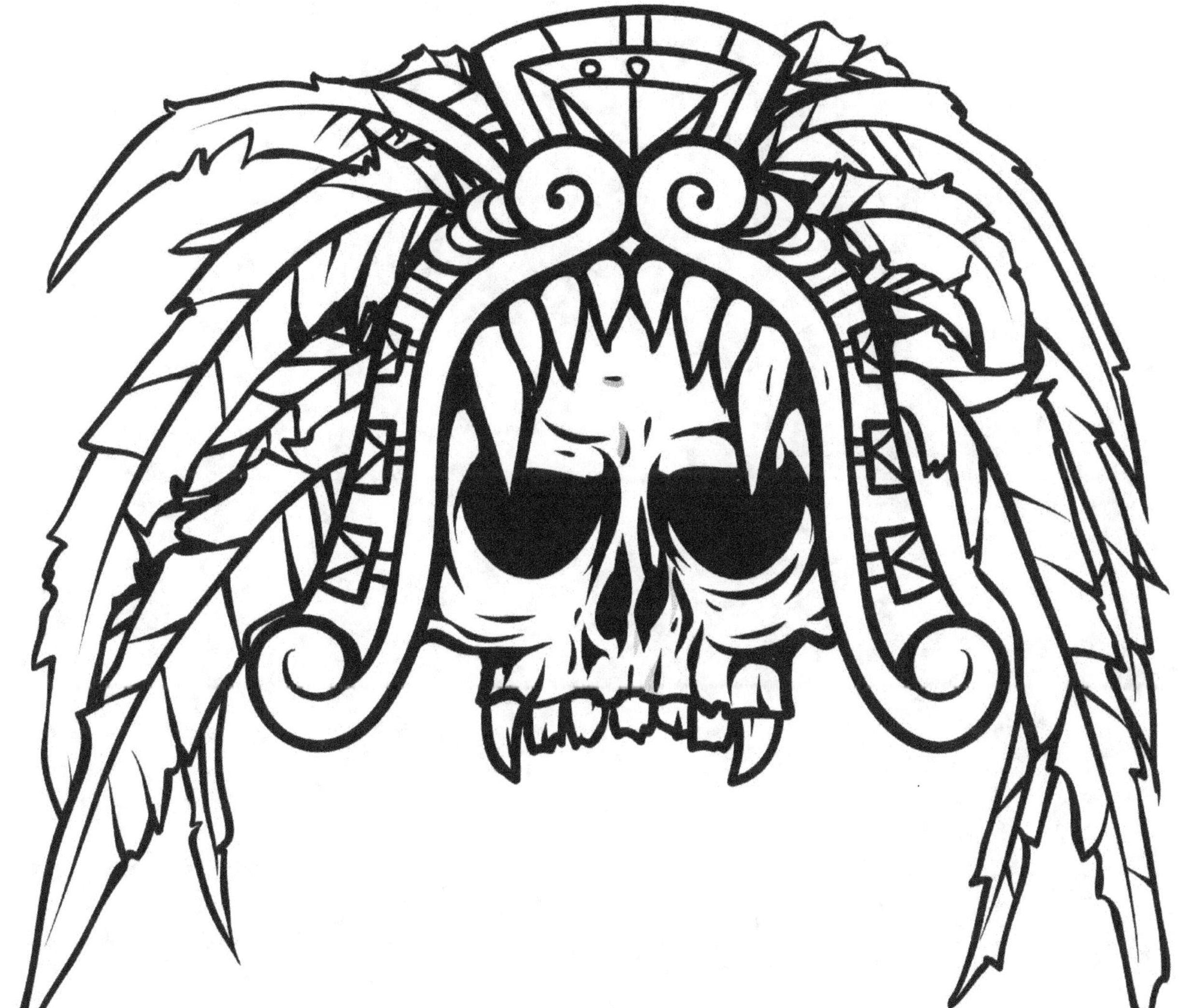

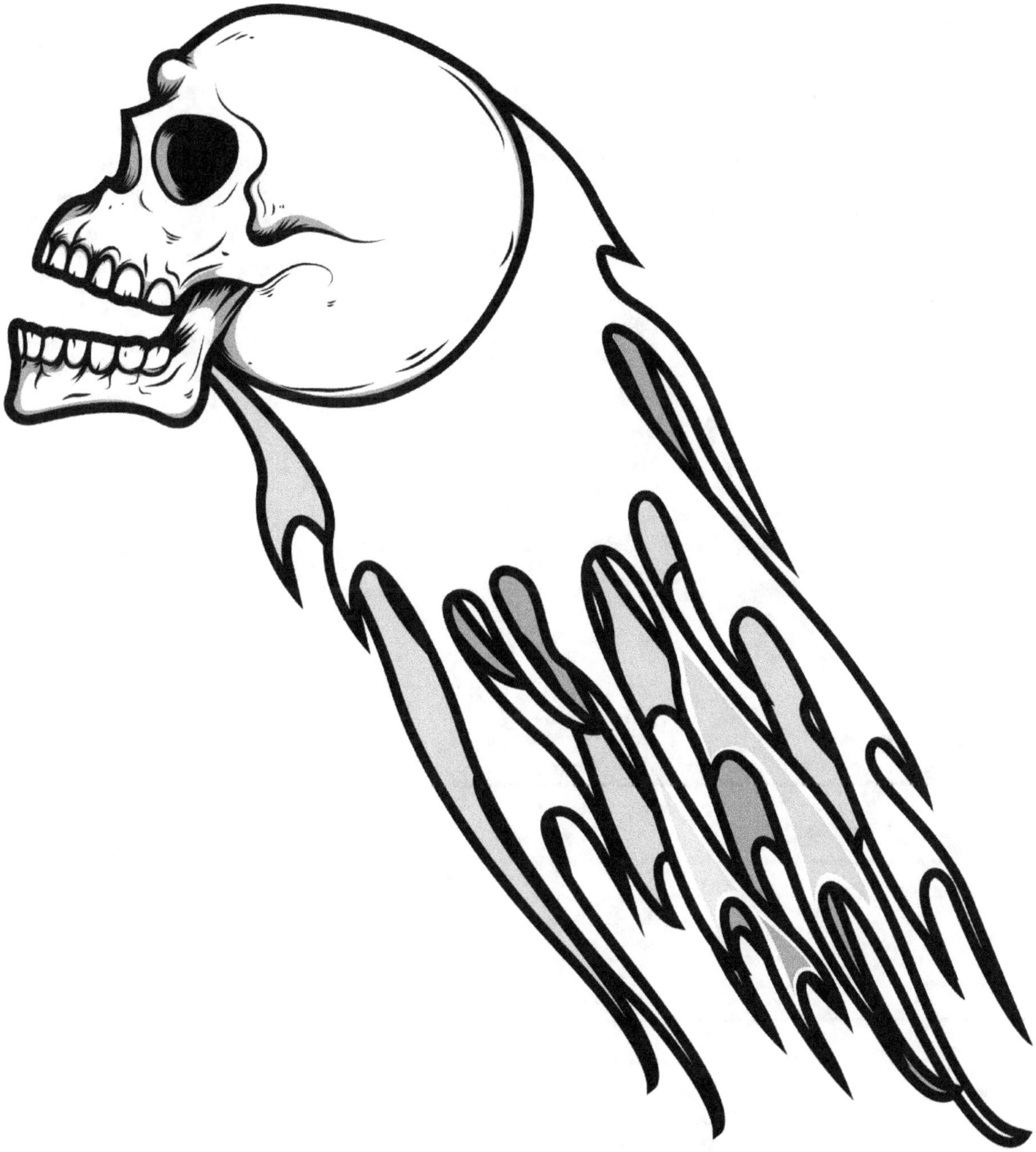

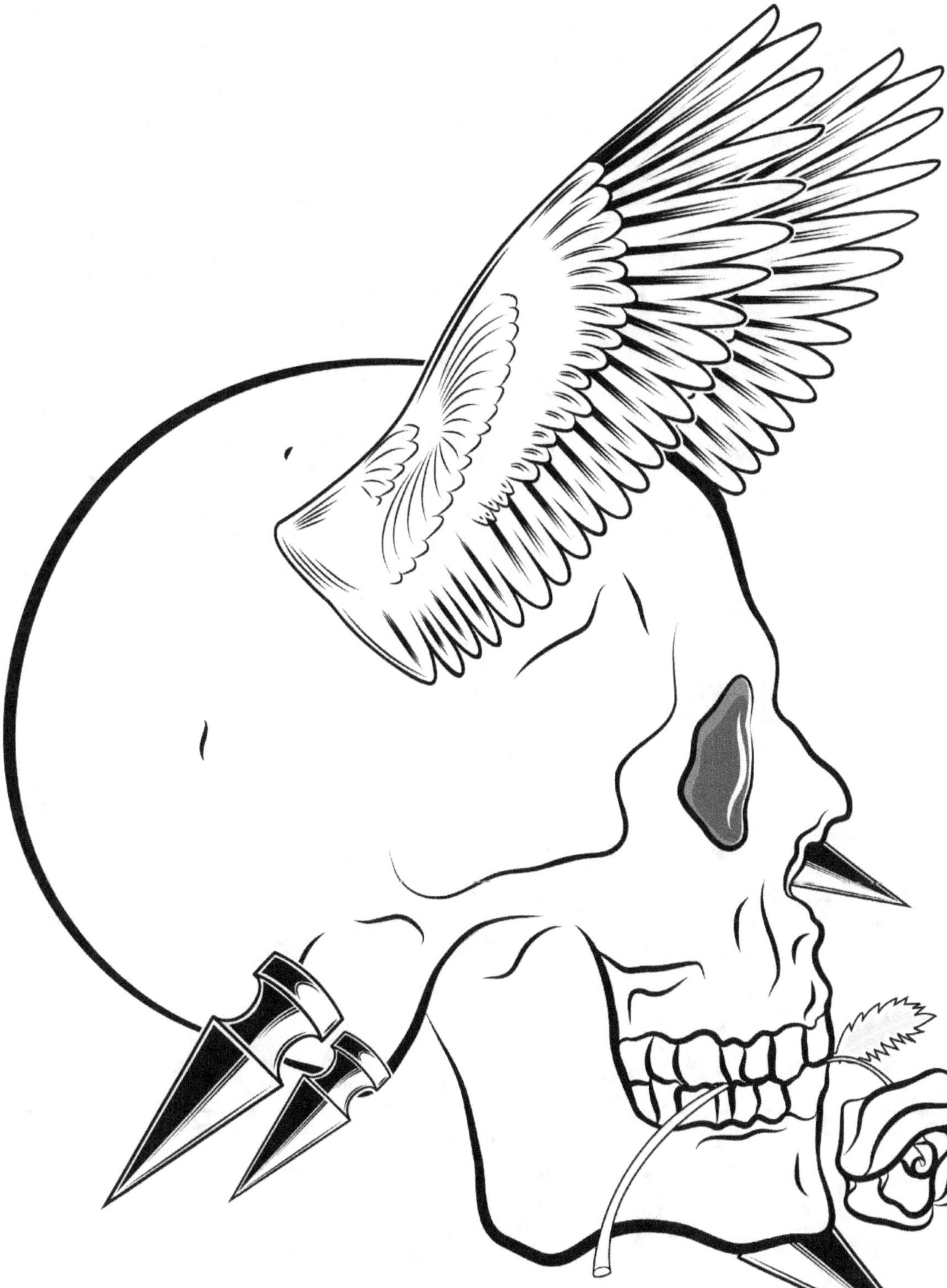

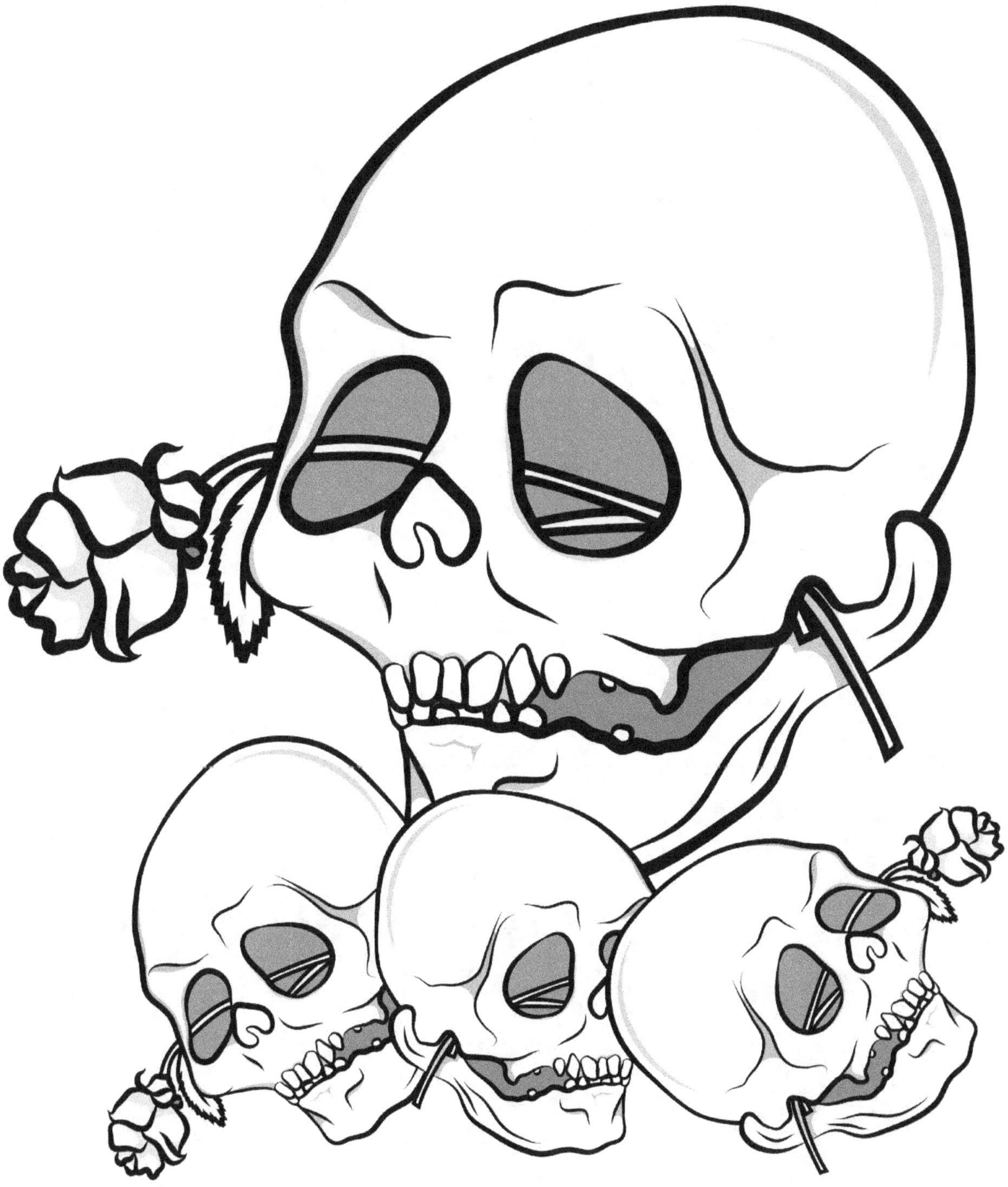

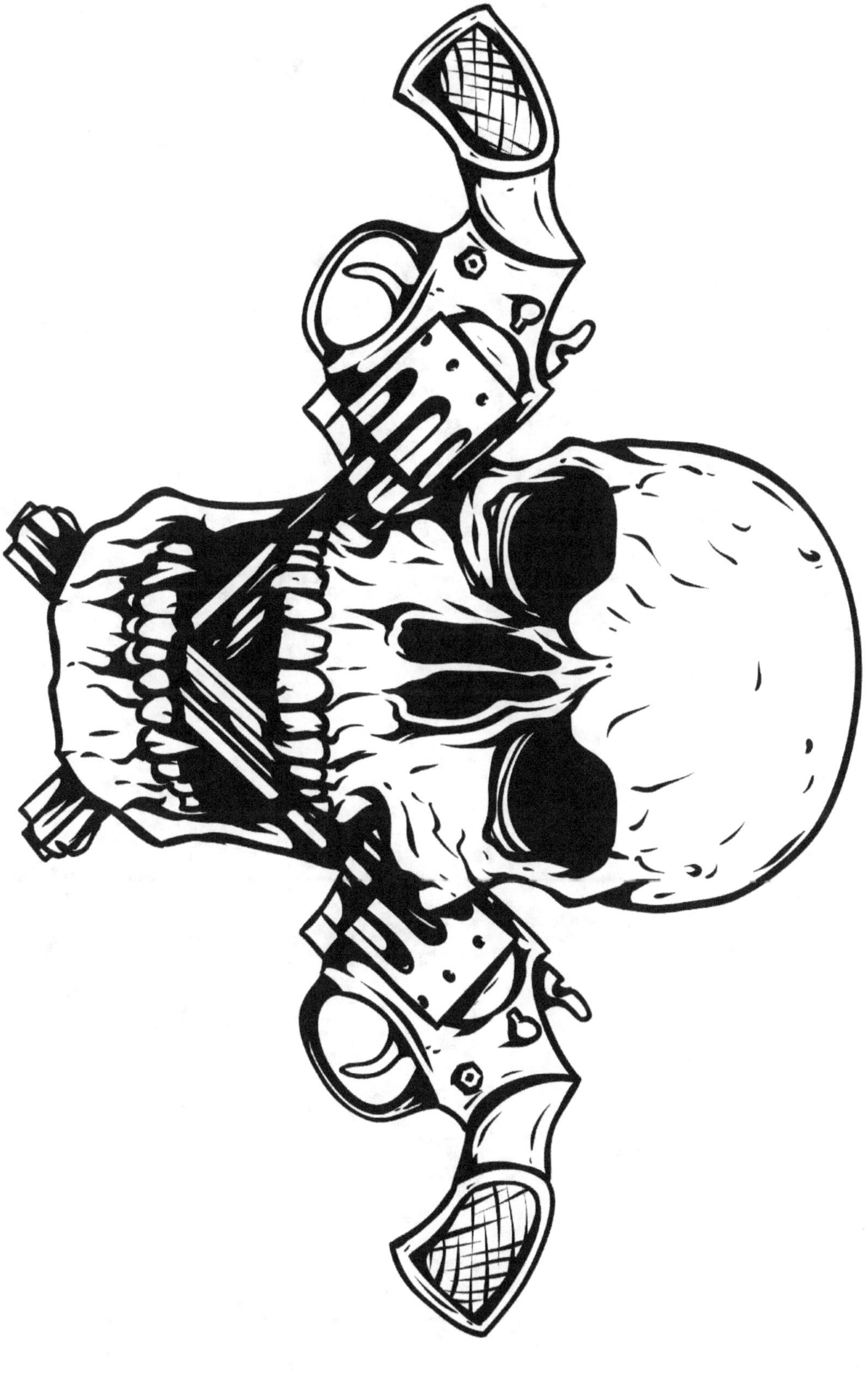

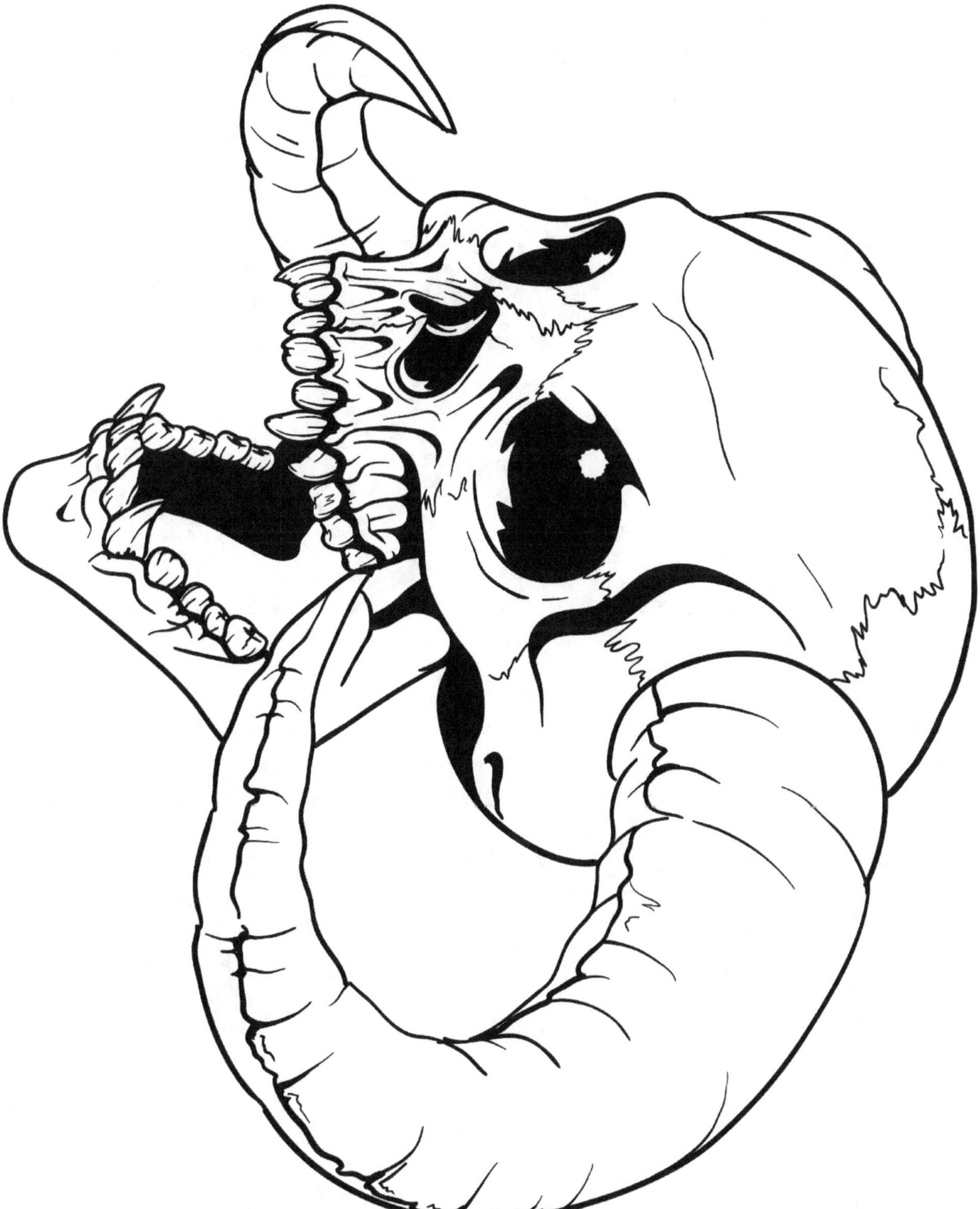

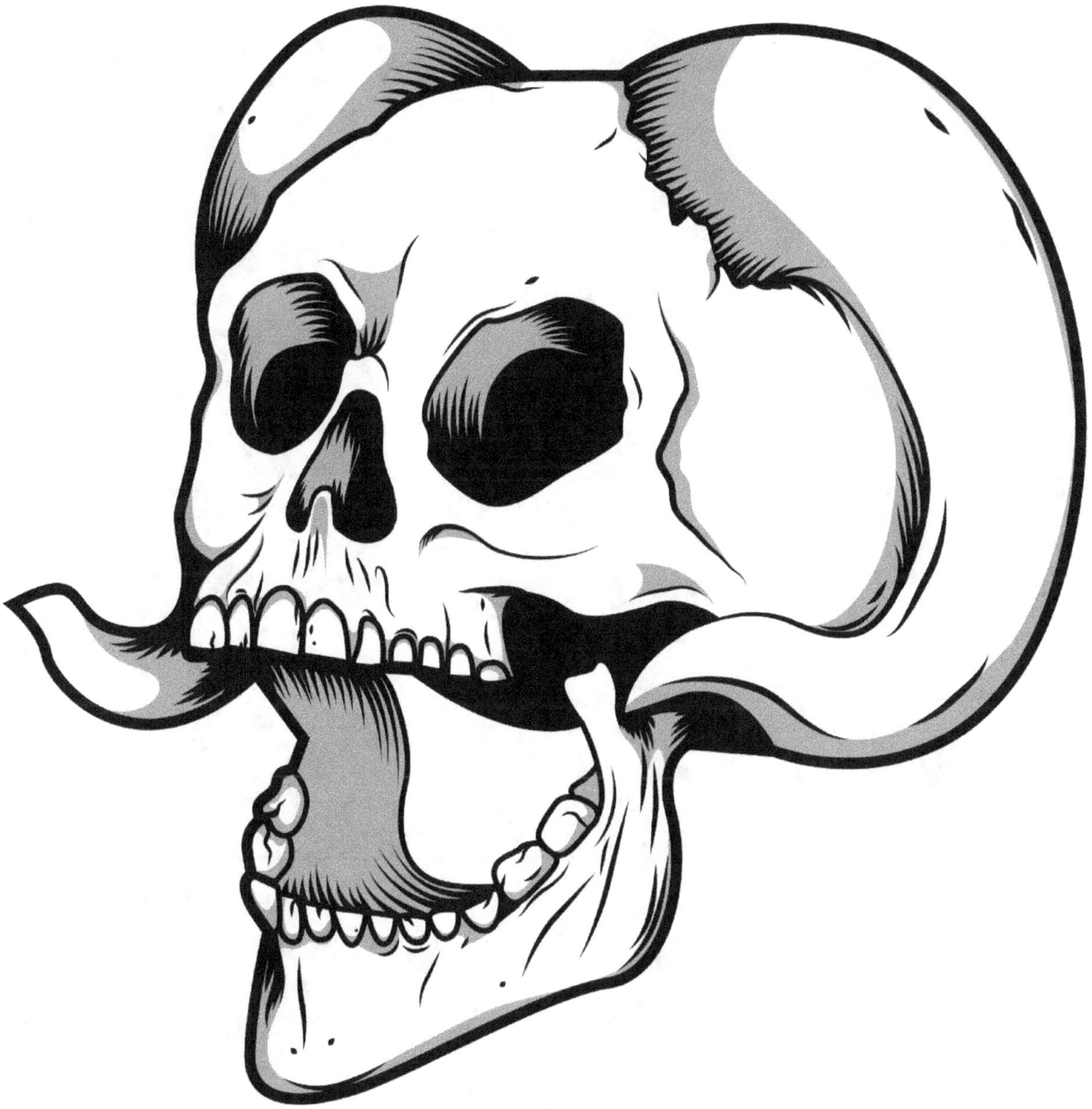

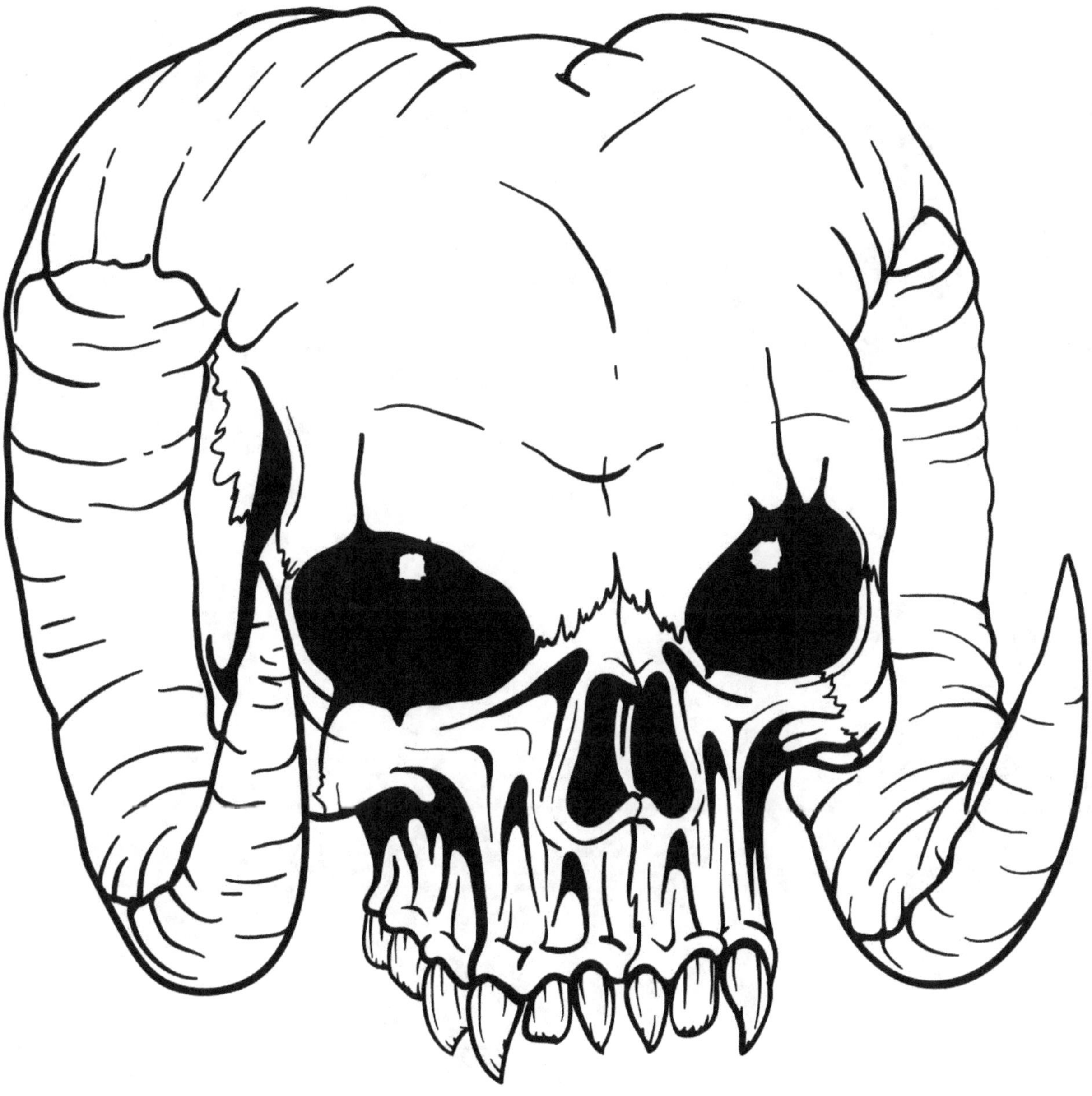

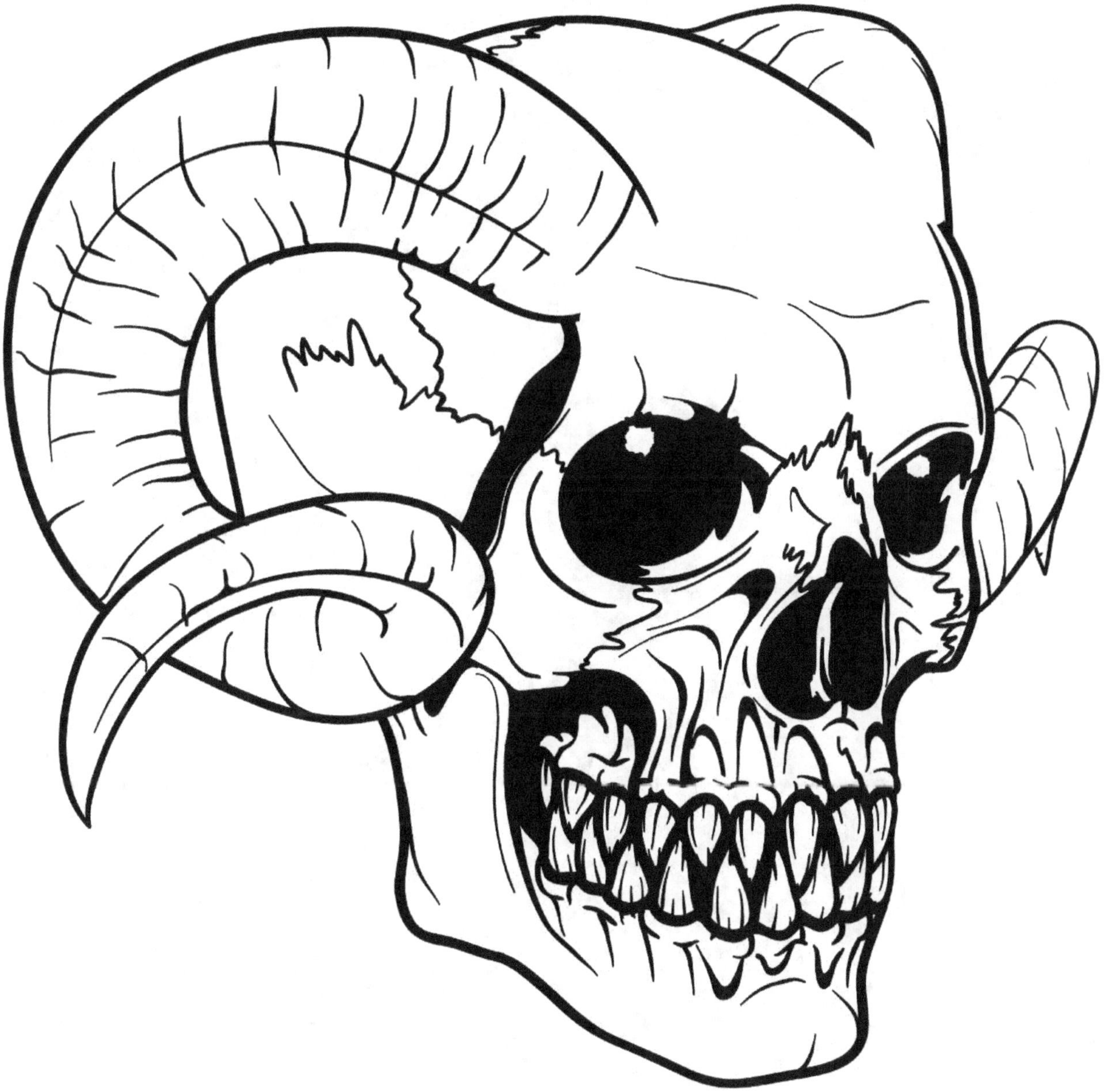

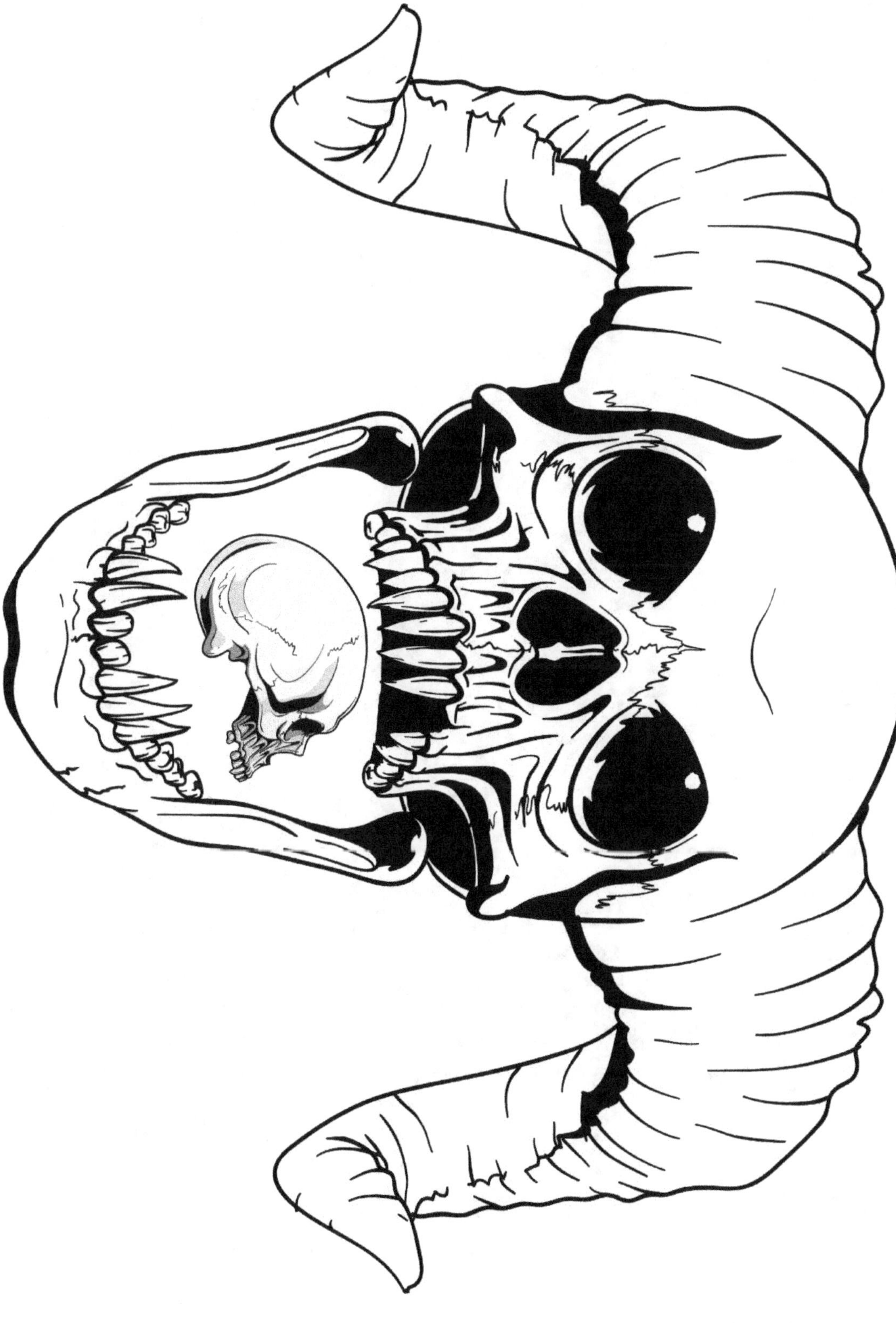

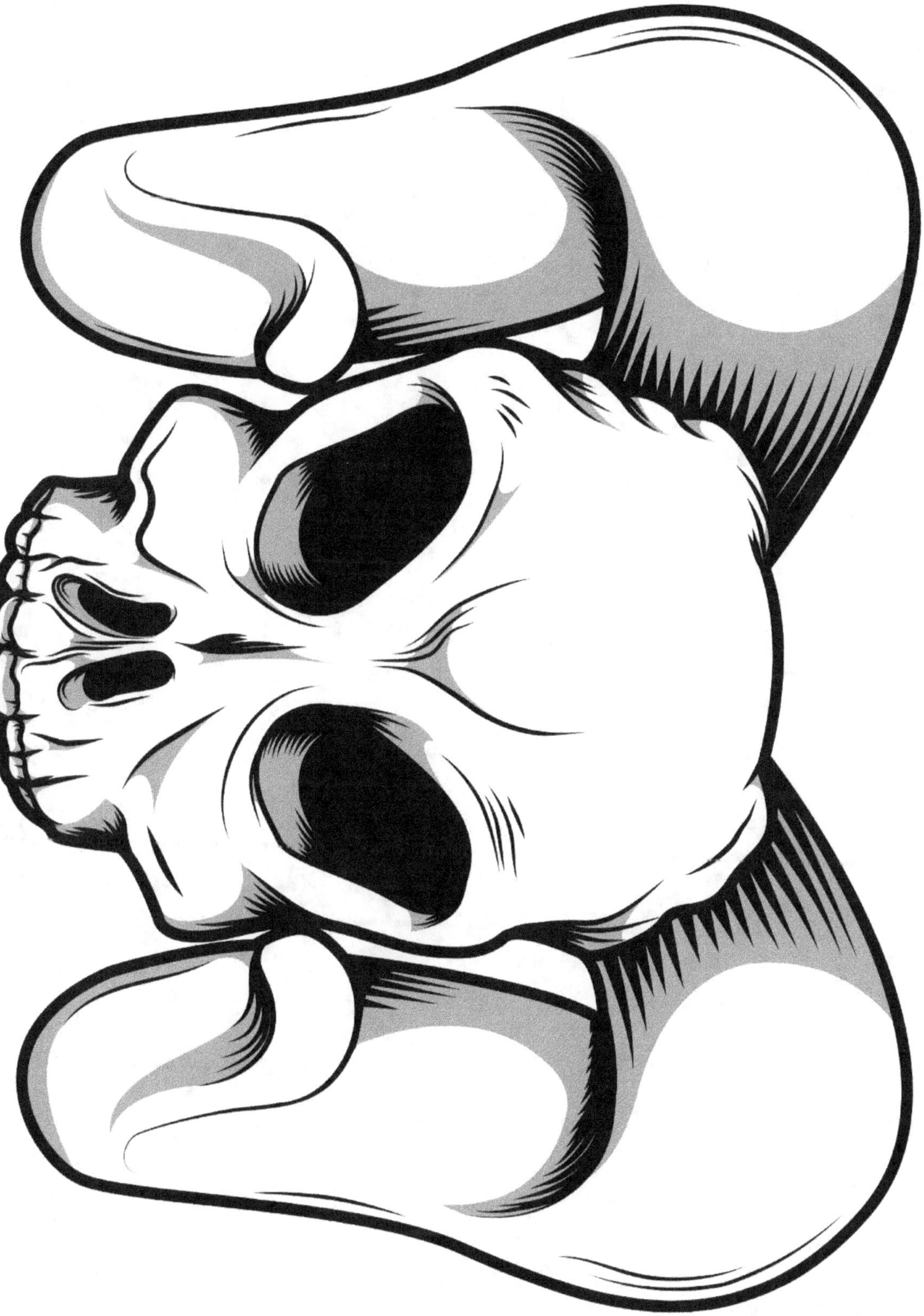

Thank You

Hope you've enjoyed your reading experience.

We here at Adult Coloring Book J. Kaiwell will always strive to deliver to you the highest quality guides.

So I'd like to thank you for supporting us and reading until the very end.

Before you go, would you mind leaving us a review on Amazon?

It will mean a lot to us and support us creating high quality guides for you in the future.

Thanks once again and here's where you can leave a review.

Warmly yours,

The Adult Coloring Book J. Kaiwell Team

www.ingramcontent.com/pod-product-compliance
Lightning Source LLC
Chambersburg PA
CBHW081135180526
45170CB00008B/3109
9781523425488